A Lenten Pilgrimage

A Lenten Pilgrimage:

Journeying with Jesus

By Archbishop J. Peter Sartain

Our Sunday Visitor Publishing Division
Our Sunday Visitor, Inc.
Huntington, Indiana 46750

Copyright © 2015 by Archbishop J. Peter Sartain. Published 2015.

20 19 18 17 16 15   1 2 3 4 5 6 7 8 9

ISBN: 978-1-61278-880-7 (Inventory No. X1675)

eISBN: 978-1-61278-884-5

Cover design: Tyler Ottinger
Cover art: Shutterstock
Interior art: Shutterstock

Printed in the United States of America

Introduction

Every Lent in the monasteries of the Orthodox Church, a seventh-century work by St. John Climacus, *The Ladder of Divine Ascent,* is read aloud to the monks. With the exception of the Bible, there is no book in Orthodox Christianity that has been studied, copied, and translated more than *The Ladder.*

John Climacus presents holiness as a ladder of thirty steps. Each rung of the ladder reflects a lesson, virtue, or grace encountered as one follows in the footsteps of Christ. I was introduced to the *Ladder* many years ago, and one passage in Step 5, "On Penitence," has always stayed with me: "Repentance is the renewal of baptism and a contract with God for a fresh start in life.... [It] is the daughter of hope and *the refusal to despair.*"

We Christians dare to look at our sinfulness only in the light of God. Repentance involves looking at myself through his eyes, with the goal of giving myself totally to him, step by step. It is a way of marveling at the greatness of God, which I can discover by admitting my smallness; it is a way of discovering God's infinite love for me, a sinner; it is the path to love-in-practice, as I learn to be as merciful to others as he is to me. In other words, repentance is not about self-improvement. It is about growth in God.

That is why John Climacus wrote, "Repentance is the refusal to despair." Through repentance, we give ourselves to God, who forgives the unforgivable debt, searches out the lost sheep, and never tires of welcoming home the wayward son or daughter.

Conversion means letting God draw us close, leaving behind those sins, attitudes, perspectives, false gods, false beliefs, and hurts that have obscured life's true purpose; it means embracing a new way of living according to the truth. Conversion unmasks the deceit of temptation and the folly of sin, and reveals

the goodness of God. It leads to spiritual growth and peace —
and it is a lifelong process.

Discovering the depths of our sin helps us see the heights
of God's love. The astounding truth is that our sinfulness occa-
sioned the outpouring of God's love in Jesus Christ, who is the
Way to fullness of life. The fruit of conversion is that we begin to
notice that being near God and living the life of Christ brings us
the fulfillment we have been unable to find any other place. We
were made for God!

My prayer is that these Lenten reflections will help you
turn toward God, grow in hope, and discover the depths and the
heights of God's mercy. Repentance is the refusal to despair.

— *Archbishop J. Peter Sartain*

Lent reveals
what's at stake

As I prayed the opening prayer at Mass for the First Sunday of Lent, I realized once again how much I have to learn:

> Grant, almighty God,
> through the yearly observances of holy Lent,
> that we may grow in understanding
> of the riches hidden in Christ
> and by worthy conduct pursue their effects.

The liturgical year continuously exposes us to every aspect of the mystery of Christ — not because we best understand his life, death, and resurrection in chronological order, but because by being continuously exposed to Christ, we allow him to enter more deeply into our lives. The same lesson I learn this year can be deepened next year, both because I have had new experiences and because I have allowed Christ to help me understand them in his light.

At the beginning of this little book, I would like to offer a "Lenten Primer" in order to outline what is at stake during this season. It seems to me that such a primer would include the following elements:

The reality of evil and of the Evil One. Satan was, at first, a good angel, created by God. But by free, deliberate choice, he and the other demons radically and irrevocably rejected God. He is a liar, who wants to draw us away from friendship with God, and it was through him that sin and death entered the world. We must face the truth that Satan exists, that he is ever on the prowl, and that we are targets of his seductions. To deny or forget that he exists, or to reduce him to a mere literary personification of evil, is to open ourselves wide to his tricks.

The recognition of original sin. We cannot tamper with the revelation of original sin without undermining our understanding of the mystery of Christ. Adam was given original holiness and justice by God — and not for himself alone, but for all human nature. He and Eve lost that grace by preferring themselves above God. By giving in to Satan's seductions, they committed a personal sin which affected the human nature they would then transmit to their descendants in a fallen state. Original sin is "contracted" and not "committed" — it is a state and not an act. This state in which we are born leaves us subject to ignorance, suffering and death, and inclined to sin.

> *"Grant, almighty God,*
> *through the yearly observances of holy Lent,*
> *that we may grow in understanding*
> *of the riches hidden in Christ*
> *and by worthy conduct pursue their effects."*

The reality of personal sin. Baptism imparts the life of Christ's grace, erases original sin, and turns us back toward God. However, the consequences of original sin (our weakened nature and inclination to sin) remain, and we confront our sinfulness in concrete situations. Lent invites us to face ourselves squarely in the mirror and admit that we have sinned — that by deliberate choice we have at times turned away from God. We cannot say, as Adam and Eve did, that "the devil made me do it." He tempted us to sin, but we take responsibility for the wrong we have done and humbly ask God and those we have offended to forgive us.

Human persons are fundamentally good. Original sin has wounded human nature but has not totally corrupted it. All of us are made in God's image and likeness — created in freedom for freedom, created in love for love. All that God created is good, and God never falls out of love for us.

The power of Satan is not infinite. Satan is only a creature and cannot prevent the building up of God's reign. He is the cause of great harm, but he cannot overpower God, whose strength and gentleness guide human and cosmic history. It is a mystery that God permits diabolical activity, but "we know that all things work for good for those who love God" (Rom 8:28). We are to fiercely avoid the ways of Satan, wisely recognize his temptations for the lies they are, and humbly cling to God. We are not equipped to battle Satan alone, and we should not try. Like Jesus, we look to our heavenly Father for strength in the fight against evil. He will keep us safe.

The Son of God saves us. God promised a redeemer to humankind, but he went beyond all expectations in sending his own Son. Jesus is the "second Adam," because in him human nature was restored to its original holiness. "Just as through one transgression condemnation came upon all, so through one righteous act acquittal and life came to all. For just as through the disobedience of one person the many were made sinners, so through the obedience of one the many will be made righteous" (Rom 5:18-19). By his death on the cross, he put an end to death's power over us.

The call to conversion. By announcing and ushering in God's reign, Jesus won back what was lost by original sin — that original holiness first enjoyed by Adam and Eve. By his death and resurrection, he set us once again on the path of God and invites us to renounce the seductions of Satan, and to give glory to his Father in all things — in heart and in action.

These are basic Christian themes which must be grasped in order to comprehend the meaning of Christ's death and resurrection, and to begin to understand how to reflect it in our lives. Next, I will explore how life gives us many opportunities to do so.

Repentance: Surrendering even our defeats to God

"**I** give up."

Depending on our circumstances and tone of voice, that phrase can mean a variety of things.

If we've been stumped by a series of good-natured questions from a friend, it can mean: "I don't know. Tell me." If we've exhausted the possibilities of a search, it can mean: "I haven't found it yet. I'm going to stop the search for now." If we feel utterly overwhelmed and beleaguered, and have neither the will nor the energy to continue, it can mean: "This thing has beaten me. I cede victory. I have been defeated."

Similarly, "to surrender" can connote a variety of things: To stop fighting because we are unable to win. To give up possession of something — "He surrendered his wallet to the thief." To let go of an idea or desire — "They surrendered the notion that they would ever hike the Appalachian Trail." To yield to a strong emotion, influence, or temptation — "He surrendered to his grief and wept bitterly." To abandon one's rights to something — "She surrendered the lease to the apartment though she had paid three months' rent in advance."

Once I used the phrase "cry uncle" in a conversation, and I was surprised that the people with whom I was speaking had never heard it. To "cry uncle" is to admit defeat, whether the game is arm wrestling or poker.

By and large, we assume that at least implicitly all of the above phrases imply that someone other than I, something other than my goal, has won. And that means I have lost. And no one likes to lose.

Will I cry uncle, lay down my defenses, and let myself be defeated? Will I sin?

Christian faith evokes a particular perspective to the dynamic of surrender and infuses it with hope. During Lent, it would be helpful to explore one aspect of that perspective as it relates to sin.

The *Catechism of the Catholic Church* defines sin as "an offense against God as well as a fault against reason, truth, and right conscience. Sin is a deliberate thought, word, deed or omission contrary to the eternal law of God" (Glossary).

In the experience of temptation, a war is waged, even if briefly, within us. Temptation creates tension and dissonance within because we instinctively recognize that something significant is at stake. We might argue, rationalize, or even lie to ourselves in the process. Will I give in to the temptation? Will I let it overpower me? Will I cry uncle, lay down my defenses, and let myself be defeated? Will I sin?

Sin is surrender to the deceptive wiles of the enemy, the devil. And that is defeat.

Repentance is surrender to the faithful love of the Friend, God. And that is victory.

There might be times when we have not only sinned but also find ourselves stuck and paralyzed in defeat, times we are tempted to give up and stop trying. To repent is to surrender even my defeat to God, whose love disarms the power of evil and the damage it has inflicted, and strengthens me to go on. To repent is to admit that on my own I cannot be victorious, but when I cling to him I am always victorious.

The good news of Christianity is that sin — the sin of Adam and Eve and our personal sin — is not the final verdict. Sin has not won, and God has not been defeated. To the contrary, on the cross Jesus gave his life as a sacrifice of atonement and reparation for our sins. He made amends for our sinful disobedience and reconciled us with our heavenly Father. By his selfless obedience and love he was victorious over sin and its most horrific damage — death — and through faith and baptism he extends his victory to us.

Surrender to God is not something to undertake only at times of temptation. The entire goal of the Christian life is to surrender everything to God. In fact, faith itself is an act of surrender.

In *Mercy in Weakness*, Cistercian Abbot André Louf writes:

"It is not the person who knows and is able to do things, who judges and condemns who practices faith. By believing, a human being yields and surrenders, lowers his arms and drops his weapons; with his whole body and all his possessions he delivers himself up to love."

God's unsurpassed love teaches us that it is always too early to give up. It is never too late to start again. It is always time to surrender to God.

In the desert we cling to essentials

A trek into the desert wilderness is no simple matter. There are hazards, privations, and loneliness; uncertainties, fickle weather, wild animals, and the frightening prospect that overnight the wind could alter the landscape beyond recognition. Because such perils lurk in the wilderness, there are rules for those who dare set foot there, rules to be followed with the utmost seriousness: Do not go it alone; take water, and lots of it; carry a compass; and wear clothes that will accommodate the changing climate.

Those who follow the rules and those who don't soon discover that the wilderness is no place for joking around, that the rumors of danger are not rumors at all but the voice of experience. It is easy to lose one's way in the wilderness.

After his baptism in the Jordan, Jesus was led by the Spirit into the desert, where after fasting for forty days and nights he was tempted by the devil.

In *Invitation to the Gospels*, Father Donald Senior writes:

"The desert held many memories for the Israelites. For Moses and their ancestors it had been a sandy bridge of rescue from the slavery of Egypt to the possibilities of freedom in a new land. But that ominous desert landscape also held memories Israel might like to forget: constant murmuring against Moses and the God he obeyed; a willingness to abandon the march and return to Egypt; despair and infidelity which led to the idolatry of a calf of gold."

The desert wilderness is that place, literally and figuratively, where what is essential (food, clothing, shelter) is made abundantly clear. Everything about life is reduced to its most basic needs: How will I live? What will I eat? For that very reason the wilderness is also a place of mirage and temptation, where we fumble about for phantom replacements for the essential. One's imagination runs wild in the wilderness, and there is no lack of forgeries posing as the real thing.

The desert wilderness is that place where what is essential is made abundantly clear.

From a spiritual perspective, the wilderness is that place we enter to be reminded of the One who is truly essential in our lives, where we stand before God with no false veneer, makeup, cologne, designer labels, or pretense. It is that place where we confront the challenges of daily life not as insurmountable problems but as steppingstones to growth. It is that place where temptation seems to hover ominously over our heads in mirages of fakes and forgeries — but where mirages collapse in the light of God's strength. It is that place where we confront ourselves with no other support than God.

The Israelites knew these things firsthand; but as Father Senior writes, they also knew that the desert was a "sandy bridge of rescue" which led to freedom. They had Moses' word that God was leading them into the desert in order to meet him, experience his unfailing love, and be taken to the land of promise.

God said constantly to them, in so many words: "Run from fakes and forgeries. Do not be fooled into believing there is anything in this world that can give you life. I alone give life, and I give it to you fully. I alone set you free. Cling to me and I will care for you. Trust in me and you will find freedom."

So it was that Jesus spent forty days and nights in the wilderness. Harassed and tempted by Satan's scams, he proved faithful to his Father and to his mission for our sakes. He showed how to prepare for the perils of the desert wilderness, for he unrelentingly clung to his Father, and to him alone. His Father was all the food, clothing, shelter, compass, and companion he needed.

And so it is for us during the forty days of voluntary wilderness living during Lent. Our penance and fasting take us to the desert, where, stripped of customary comforts and excess, we learn to rely on God alone. In prayer he proves a faithful companion and guide who helps us see our perils and ourselves in clear relief. It is Jesus who shows the way by exposing the machinations of the devil as slick fakery. It is Jesus who shows how to be patient and obedient when the perils lurking in our personal wilderness seem overwhelming. It is Jesus who is the bridge, not made of sand but of love, that takes us safely to freedom.

Not all our forays into the wilderness are voluntary, and most of them do not wait for Lent to unsettle or frighten us. There is the desert of illness, of joblessness, of loneliness, of anxiety, of conflict, and of doubt; the wilderness of moving to a new town and a new job, or grieving the loss of a spouse or a child, or getting back on one's feet after bewildering setbacks. Lent reminds us that though any wilderness can shake us to our bones, it can also reveal the bridge, the comfort, the rock, the strength, and the freedom who is Jesus.

> "Blessed be the LORD, my rock,
>   who trains my hands for battle,
>   my fingers for war;
> My safeguard and my fortress,
>   my stronghold, my deliverer,
> My shield, in whom I take refuge" (Ps 144:1-2).

Taming our distractions
with loving desire

Watching cable television news, I am amazed at the amount of information streaming across the screen — weather forecasts, sports scores, stock market quotes, headlines about a wide range of stories. Each stream distracts from the others, making it difficult to focus on any of them. Each network competes with the others using high-tech distractions.

Have we become so mesmerized by diversions and distractions that they have become the point? The sheer volume of news and entertainment available at the flip of a switch seems to say that it is better to be distracted than focused.

I can conjure up enough distractions on my own, without any help from the media. I am distracted in prayer, in work, in reading, in driving, in conversation. I am distracted by hunger, by worry, by noise, by snow, by fatigue.

Sometimes people think it would be easier to avoid distractions if one joined a monastery. Poor Clare nuns and Benedictine or Trappist monks would quickly tell us otherwise. Distractions follow us wherever we go.

Distractions are an inevitable part of every person's life, but they are not the point of life. They enticingly pose as something — anything — that promises what it cannot deliver: nourishment. In fact, if we constantly allow ourselves to bump from one distraction to another, we will never be at peace, and we will never find fulfillment. This is particularly true when we allow distractions to derail our relationship with God. The problem is that initially harmless distractions can attract our wills away from what is good and cause us to do what is evil.

During Lent we deliberately go to the desert with Jesus — not to escape anything or anyone, but to seek the Father.

The First Sunday of Lent turned our attention to Jesus' forty days' retreat into the desert, where he was tempted. Satan's goal was to exploit his hunger pangs in order to distract him from the Father, to trick him into going for the quick fix, to nudge him into claiming all the glory as his own. Though buffeted by Satan's empty promises, Jesus remained grounded in his relationship with the Father, which he preferred to everything the world could offer.

We live at a time when distractions and temptations within are compounded by those constantly aimed at us from without. Thus during Lent we deliberately go to the desert with Jesus — not to escape anything or anyone, but to seek the Father. We have allowed ourselves to be distracted by many things that have often kept us from our responsibilities and our spiritual lives. Some have led us to sin. We will never rid ourselves of all distractions and temptations, but we can deliberately shed some of them. Fasting, giving alms, and praying are steps in that direction.

Fasting and abstaining from meat make us hungry, but in truth those disciplines are just a small glimpse of what our Savior sacrificed for us. Almsgiving calls us away from selfish preoccupations and spurs us to active love for those who are hungry not because they have chosen to fast, but because they have no food. Prayer is the bread that feeds us, because it comes from the hand of the Father.

The nagging hunger pangs we feel during Lent are a helpful tool, for the desire for food is a symbolic reminder of the most basic human hunger — the hunger for a nourishing, intimate friendship with God. We hunger for it precisely because God extends his hand toward us. Distractions are the junk food we use as a substitute. Temptations are Satan's ploy to discourage us and damage that friendship through sin.

Is the point of Lent to focus on God by concentrating with furrowed brows, gritting our teeth, and clinching our fists in fierce determination not to be distracted or tempted? Definitely not! Most of us have found that such effort soon ends in frustration. Focusing on God is not so much a matter of concentration as it is of loving desire. When a sparse Lenten lunch makes us hungry at about 2:00 p.m., we can say, "Lord, thank you for reminding me that it is really for you that I am hungry." When thoughts too numerous to count distract us, we can say, "Jesus, I love you," and let them pass in and out of our minds, disarming them of their influence. When temptation threatens to draw our wills from friendship with God, we can say, "I worship and serve only you, my God."

Lent gives us the opportunity and the means to focus on the "one thing" necessary (see Lk 10:38-42), even in the midst of all that churns within and around us. It is our forty-day retreat into the desert to be with the Father. Ironically, we get our bearings in the desert not by any map or skill of ours but by our helplessness and hunger. We will be distracted and tempted even there, but the Father is there, awaiting us. He is unfailingly present to us in spite of all that may be going through our minds and hearts. If he were not, we would cease to exist.

To whom else can we go? Our deepest hunger is for him.

Coming home to the loving embrace of the Father

Commenting on the parable of the prodigal son, Father Carroll Stuhlmueller once wrote: "The most difficult of reconciliations is always between relatives who have been split apart by money, scandal, and wasteful living. Civil wars are always the bloodiest with the deepest scars."

When public television aired Ken Burns' celebrated series on the U.S. Civil War several years ago, we were reminded that our own American past was marred by such pain not that long ago. The wounds were deep and long lasting. And most of us can quickly scan our family history and discover uncomfortable, unhealed hurts.

The head of the family — mother, father, matriarch, patriarch — is often the one who feels most acutely the pain of family division; but all family members, even if not involved directly in the conflict, are affected by it in some way. We tiptoe around certain topics, feel ill at ease in someone's presence, try to find ways of avoiding awkward situations.

Jesus' parable of the prodigal son is appealing because family conflicts are both familiar and always aching to be healed. At different times in our lives we have probably acted all the parts in the parable. Perhaps we were once the wayward child who pouted and whined and squandered family resources; or, again, we were the faithful child who resented the lenient treatment our wayward sibling received; or we were the forgiving parent who did not care who did what, or how much it cost, but simply rejoiced that we were a family again.

God loves both the faithful and the wayward, and he never takes his eyes off those who have run away.

The way Jesus tells it, the central character in the parable is actually the forgiving father — "prodigal" himself because he is recklessly wasteful and extravagant with forgiveness. God loves both the faithful and the wayward, and he never takes his eyes off those who have run away. Even as the prodigal son is wasting his inheritance on evil, his father is awaiting his return; after all, he knows what his son is missing by being separated from the family. And when the elder son protests that the father's mercy is undeserved and unfair, the father responds with a wonderful word of love that embraced them both:

"My son, you are here with me always; everything I have is yours. But now we must celebrate and rejoice, because your brother was dead and has come to life again; he was lost and has been found" (Lk 15:31-32).

Paul wrote, "God was reconciling the world to himself in Christ, not counting their trespasses against them and entrusting to us the message of reconciliation" (2 Cor 5:19). We are often still the prodigal children who waste our moments on evil — but God will always be the prodigal Father ready to lavish his mercy on us. He knows that sin hurts and divides us, and he wants us to be healed and free.

The Sacrament of Penance is available throughout the year, but during Lent we highlight its crucial place in the life of the Church. God is still reconciling the world to himself through Christ! He knows well our divided hearts and divided families; he knows our need and yearning for forgiveness; he knows that we suffer when we have sinned.

Haven't all parents wanted to embrace their children when they have painfully come to the realization that they sinned — or wanted to embrace them even before they came to that realization, hoping that the embrace itself would have an effect? And haven't they wanted to hug them all the more when they backed away?

God has watched us tiptoe around him and around others — those we have hurt or those who have hurt us. He has watched us wastefully slip into sin. He has watched us cause division, and he has seen how we have been injured by someone else's war.

He has watched us fall unquestioningly in line with the ways of the world. He knows that those ways will never satisfy us, but that his ways will. He knows that his mercy will bring us peace and heal our fractured lives, and thus he offers the Sacrament of Penance as a means of returning to his loving embrace.

We offer many reasons for not going to confession: "It's been so long, I wouldn't know where to begin." "Why ask forgiveness if I think I might sin again because of a habit I find hard to break?" "Why confess to a priest? I would rather just tell my sins privately to God." "I don't know what sin is anymore." "I'm too embarrassed to tell anyone what I have done, and I am afraid God will not forgive me." "The confession schedule is not convenient for me."

Hearing our hesitations and excuses, our heavenly Father still awaits us. He aches to forgive us, because he knows what we miss when estranged — and he knows that perhaps we have forgotten what it feels like to be forgiven and freed.

Has it been a while since you went to confession? Your prodigal Father is waiting to lavish his mercy on you through his Son.

One lesson of Lent:
God alone is enough

Lenten seasons long ago, my parents taught us to recognize that many things we considered essential to daily life — especially favorite foods and entertainments — were, in fact, secondary and that we could live without them with just a little effort. I often groaned in compliance with Lent's penances. But even though their full meaning escaped me in those days, they made a lasting impression. I knew Lent was important. I knew God was important.

I once had a parishioner who was not in the habit of going to Sunday Mass. His wife and I good-naturedly chided him about his Sunday obligation, but he knew we were serious. He makes special effort from time to time, but inevitably he slides off track again. One Lent, however, he resolved to start going to Mass every Sunday without fail. He sent me this email message:

"Bishop Sartain, as my Lenten resolution, I decided to start going to Mass every Sunday. But the other day, my wife told me that the Sundays of Lent are not days of penance. Does that mean I should not go to Mass?"

Nice try, I wrote him. An obligation is an obligation. My friend was kidding, of course, but his humor does offer insight into the purpose of Lenten sacrifices and resolutions. Why do we fast, abstain, and make sacrifices during Lent? There are a variety of reasons.

The first and most important reason is this: God alone is enough. This insight dawned on me only gradually as I grew older, started paying attention to my relationship with God, and realized that I literally would not survive without him. I learned that God is not a lifeline to be used as a last resort; he is, in fact, everything, whether things are going well or badly. One reason we fast and abstain and make sacrifices in Lent — in other words, one reason we "do without" — is so that we can focus on the One we cannot do without.

It is easy to delude ourselves into thinking that we need many things and forget that, as Jesus told Martha, "There is need of only one thing."

If we truly want to focus on God, it is helpful and even necessary to peel away layers of comfort and excess to arrive at the kernel of life. It is easy to delude ourselves into thinking that we need many things and forget that, as Jesus told Martha, "There is need of only one thing" (Lk 10:42). Lent's fasting, abstinence, and sacrifices remind us to place our focus there.

"Obligation" is a concept not always appreciated in our culture. We have an obligation to participate in Mass every Sunday and holy day of obligation, an obligation to receive holy Communion at least during the Easter season, and an obligation to confess our grave sins at least once each year. These are three of the Precepts of the Church.

Obligation is not a dirty word. In fact, these obligations ensure that we avail ourselves of the great blessings of the Church — the Eucharist and God's loving mercy. Why would one not want to fulfill such "obligations" when they point us in the direction of the one thing necessary, the direction of the One without whom we cannot live?

We owe God the fulfillment of religious obligations, in grateful response for what he has done for us. They are truly the least we could do.

There is another, more subtle benefit to the sacrifices and penances of Lent: They help us grow in trust. Perhaps that sounds strange. But when we take such tangible steps to say to ourselves, "I cannot live without God," we see unmistakably that he supplies all our needs and is worthy of our trust. It is good for us to expose the excesses we have come to regard as necessities, because doing so unveils the only One who is a necessity. We understand that it has not been creature comforts that have sustained us through life, but God. God alone.

The obligations to which we are subject as Catholics are not ends in themselves. The true objective is for the observing of them to become so natural in us that it would never occur to us not to observe them. When obligations "disappear" in that way, we begin to understand that the very air we breathe comes from God.

In the sixteenth century, St. Teresa of Ávila once jotted some verses in her breviary, which were translated from the Spanish in the nineteenth century by Henry Wadsworth Longfellow:

> Let nothing disturb thee,
> Nothing affright thee
> All things are passing;
> God never changeth;
> Patient endurance
> Attaineth to all things;
> Who God possesseth
> In nothing is wanting;
> Alone God sufficeth.

Thank God for Lent, for penance, for abstinence from meat, for fasting, for sacrifices, for obligations. Without them we might drown in the delusion that we need many things. Alone God sufficeth.

How large is my emotional footprint?

I am surprised there are any functioning pedestrian street-crossing buttons in Seattle, considering the way we mistreat them. Since I walk to the office most days, I cross a number of streets, often amid heavy traffic, and I make frequent use of those sturdy-looking metal buttons.

One day, it dawned on me that I often pressed the button twice — for emphasis, I suppose, or in the vain hope that doing so would speed things up. Then I began to notice that other people did the same, and that often they hammer the button with their fists so ferociously that it's a wonder it even works (I read that in some cities the buttons are purposely deactivated).

When I realized that my habit of pushing the button twice was irrational, I stopped doing so. I figured a little less violence toward an inanimate object, and a little less insistence on my presence, would do Seattle and its traffic technology some good.

Years ago I decided that when flying I would always request an aisle seat. I've flown so much that looking out the window no longer holds fascination for me, and I am always uncomfortable asking others to leave their seats if I am sitting by the window and need a break.

If an aisle seat is not available, a window seat will do, but a middle seat is another matter. I am not typically claustrophobic, but finding myself crammed between two other passengers is an experience I never enjoy. Which arm rest should I use? Am I allowed to use either? Neither? Both? Thus a personal rule: Avoid middle seats at all cost.

How often do I make the world around me revolve around me?

The way one uses the space around his or her seat on an airplane varies greatly from person to person. One's size is not the determining factor in how much space he or she occupies. Small people using both armrests, leaning erratically from side to side, stretching their legs into their neighbor's legroom, listening to music audible despite earphones, and speaking loudly on cellphones, take up a lot of space. I may be sitting on the aisle, but if seated next to such people, I feel cramped. Do they realize someone is sitting next to them?

Much is made these days of one's "carbon footprint" — a calculation of how much carbon dioxide one adds to the atmosphere through the consumption of fossil fuels (driving a certain car, using a certain amount of electricity, flying a certain number of miles, adjusting the thermostat to a certain temperature, and so forth). I wonder what would happen if we also took stock of our "emotional footprint" — the effect we have on others by the bluster of our moods, the amount of space we occupy when oblivious to those around us, the volume and pitch of our opinions and complaints, the weight we give to our very presence?

I have a feeling that if we took stock of that "emotional footprint," we might back off just a bit. In fact, taking such an inventory could be a good Lenten exercise.

How often do I make the world around me revolve around me?

Would those with whom I live and work, if I gave them the opportunity to speak, say that I am a force to contend with, a physical and emotional presence not easily accommodated?

Do I say loudly things that would be better said softly? Do I speak when silence would be more appropriate and more welcome?

Do I take up so much emotional space that my family, friends, and co-workers are overwhelmed and intimidated?

Do I sap the energy and mood from a room by my bad-tempered attitude?

Do I hang up the phone harshly, slam the door excessively, push the traffic signal button too fiercely?

I have a hunch that if each of us would ask such simple questions, the mood around us would lighten, and a smile would return to our faces.

Why is such a simple inventory appropriate to Lent? The Letter of James offers some hints:

"If anyone does not fall short in speech, he is a perfect man, able to bridle his whole body also. If we put bits into the mouths of horses to make them obey us, we also guide their whole bodies. It is the same with ships: even though they are so large and driven by fierce winds, they are steered by a very small rudder wherever the pilot's inclination wishes. In the same way the tongue is a small member and yet has great pretensions. Consider how small a fire can set a huge forest ablaze" (Jas 3:2-5).

"Who among you is wise and understanding? Let him show his works by a good life in the humility that comes from wisdom. But if you have bitter jealousy and selfish ambition in your hearts, do not boast and be false to the truth. Wisdom of this kind does not come down from above but is earthly, unspiritual, demonic. For where jealousy and selfish ambition exist, there is disorder and every foul practice. But the wisdom from above is first of all pure, then peaceable, gentle, compliant, full of mercy and good fruits, without inconstancy or insincerity. And the fruit of righteousness is sown in peace for those who cultivate peace" (3:13-18).

This Lent, may we resolve to leave a smaller emotional footprint and cultivate peace: peace in our homes, peace at work, peace on the streets, peace in our hearts. But not our peace — God's peace.

Opening ourselves to God's immeasurable mercy

Growing up at our house meant sharing chores and treats, and the definition of "sharing" was sometimes taken to extremes by us kids.

Washing and drying supper dishes was a job for all five of us. As the youngest, I didn't have to wash, but I was expected to dry, usually sharing the task with one of my sisters. Drying dishes was not difficult, but it interfered with playing and TV. It seemed to me that the best way to be fair was to count the wet dishes and silverware. I would dry half, and she would dry half. Exactly half.

Pepsi was the cola of choice in our family, most especially because it was my father's favorite. The Pepsi bill was not small for our family of seven, and most of the time we asked permission only to "split a Pepsi." Split meant split, so we took the measuring cup and carefully poured out five ounces from the ten-ounce bottle to ensure that no one was slighted.

To tell the truth, the balance of work and worry at our house was indisputably lopsided, with my parents always carrying the heaviest load. Mom did most of the chores, and there were many things we did not feel the need to "split" (I don't remember any arguments over broccoli or mashed potatoes). As lopsided as things were in our favor, the way we kids saw it, measuring was necessary to ensure that none of us was personally overburdened or personally underprivileged.

One time, a high school friend, angered for some reason by our biology teacher, announced that she would get back at him by failing the next test. Who was more punished by that revenge?

At times our sense of egalitarianism is carried to extremes, and when life is not fair as we define "fair," we brood.

Other folks have told me similar stories about growing up at their house and school. We laugh about the past and our childhood sense of justice, but perhaps we also recognize that as adults we still take ridiculously precise measurements in other areas of life, or refuse to let go of measurements we took long ago. At times our sense of egalitarianism is carried to extremes, and when life is not fair as we define "fair," we brood.

We compare the success of others to our perceived lack of good fortune and grind our teeth. We observe their looks, their possessions, their friends, and count ourselves short. We forgive little when we have been forgiven much. We count so obsessively what we do have that we fail to figure how we have more than enough to share with the needy. We gauge the length and height and weight of injuries inflicted on us, and don't recognize that it is our need to settle scores that injures us most.

Luckily, God does not measure as we measure, nor does he expect that we carry an equal share of the burden he bears for us. He does not measure our sins as they could easily be measured, nor does he hold back his love, though our love for him is puny in comparison. He does not stop sharing with us when we are stingy with others, nor does he retaliate, as we are sometimes tempted to do. In our relationship with God, everything is undeniably lopsided in our favor by his mercy. We keep count and measure, but he never stops lavishing his love, his forgiveness, his favor.

Two familiar responsorial psalms are eloquent reminders of this truth: "If you, O Lord, mark iniquities, Lord, who can stand?" "Lord, do not deal with us according to our sins."

If there were a measuring contest, and the scale of our iniquities would be compared to the scale of God's goodness, none of us could "stand." If God dealt with us "equitably" as our sins deserve, we would never know the length and depth and height and breadth of his mercy.

God does not measure as we measure, or compare as we compare. He is pure goodness, pure love. He is the One who bears the burden without counting, simply because we are his beloved. Any sharing that is done is done by him. Even when he invites us to "take up your cross," it is only so that we will experience the power of his love as he bears its crushing weight, only so that we will learn how to put his love into action.

Oliver Lyttelton, a British businessman who entered government service during World War II, once said of Winston Churchill, "He seldom carries forward from the ledger of today into tomorrow's account." Such an admirable human trait reminds us that God never carries forward from yesterday's ledger. He doesn't even keep a ledger.

May we open ourselves to God's unfathomable, literally immeasurable, forgiveness. Coming to terms with his mercy changes us forever. Through contact with him may you and your loved ones be unburdened and unfettered, freed of scales and measuring cups, secure and at peace in his nearness.

"Not as man sees does God see, because man sees the appearance but the Lord looks into the heart" (1 Sm 16:7, NAB).

Fed and nourished for the paschal journey

Spiritually, we are constantly going and coming from Jerusalem. Jerusalem has always been considered a sacred place, a holy city chosen by God for his throne, his dwelling place among his people, the center point from which salvation radiates. Its Temple was considered extraordinarily sacred, a place of attachment and spiritual identity for every Jew.

Jesus went there many times. As a child, he was presented to the Lord in the Temple, and it was there that Simeon told Mary her heart would be pierced as though by a sword. Each year Mary and Joseph went to Jerusalem for Passover, and Jesus accompanied them. When he was twelve, on the journey home his parents discovered with horror that he was not with them. They later found him back in the Temple — he called it his "Father's house" — discussing religious matters with the teachers.

During Jesus' forty days in the desert, Satan led him to the parapet of the Temple and tempted him to display his divinity by jumping off so angels would catch him, but Jesus would have none of it. "You should not put the Lord, your God, to the test," he told the devil.

In Luke and the Acts of the Apostles, Jerusalem is the point toward which Jesus is constantly moving and the hub from which the preaching of the Gospel goes out to the world. Luke reaches a critical climax in Chapter 9 when Jesus determines to go to Jerusalem: "When the days for his being taken up were fulfilled, he resolutely determined to journey to Jerusalem" (v. 51). The chapters that follow are marked by the determination and tension that met Jesus' courageous decision.

"I must continue on my way today, tomorrow, and the following day, for it is impossible that a prophet should die outside of Jerusalem."

Many thought he should not go. Some of his disciples were frightened for him and not a little for themselves. He continued to teach and heal along the way, heightening the antipathy some felt for him and affirming his insight that something definitive would happen there. Some of the Pharisees warned him to go away because Herod wanted to kill him, but Jesus replied:

"Go and tell that fox, 'Behold, I cast out demons and I perform healings today and tomorrow, and on the third day I accomplish my purpose. Yet I must continue on my way today, tomorrow, and the following day, for it is impossible that a prophet should die outside of Jerusalem'" (Lk 13:32-33).

Moved by the ache in his heart for the holy city that had rejected him, he added, "Jerusalem, Jerusalem, you who kill the prophets and stone those sent to you, how many times I yearned to gather your children together as a hen gathers her brood under her wings, but you were unwilling!" (13:34).

Jesus loved Jerusalem and her people, and it distressed him that many were rejecting him. He continued his journey nonetheless, a final journey to his death.

After his death, some of his disciples left Jerusalem. Disappointed and disillusioned, hopelessly licking their wounds, they headed back to their former lives. The Gospel of Luke recounts the beautiful story of two disciples who encountered Jesus on the road to Emmaus — the road away from Jerusalem — and how he asked where they were going and what had happened to make them so sad. They did not recognize him, but he explained the Scriptures and blessed and broke bread with them, just as he had done at the Last Supper. Their eyes were opened, and they returned to Jerusalem full of hope in the risen Lord (see 24:13-35).

Spiritually, we are constantly going and coming from Jerusalem. There is a learning curve to discipleship, and we alternate between fervor and sluggishness, conviction and doubt, hope and hesitation. One day we are zealously determined to make the journey to Jerusalem with Jesus no matter the cost — to take up our cross and suffer with him, to stand up for the faith and live only for him. The next day, when something unnerving happens, we hesitate and head in the opposite direction, away from the cross and toward Emmaus.

But Jesus catches up with us, too, not at all surprised that fear of the cross has gotten the best of us. "What are you thinking as you walk away?" he gently questions. If we pour out our hearts to him in prayer and listen to his word, he opens our eyes and gives us strength for the return trip.

And he feeds us. In every sense, the Eucharist is food for the journey, as Luke's account of the meeting on the road to Emmaus unmistakably illustrates. Wherever we find ourselves spiritually — walking toward or away from Jerusalem — we need the nourishment of the Lord's Body and Blood.

The Eucharist keeps us strong for our journey to Jerusalem, because it is a participation in Jesus' sacrifice on the cross and a share in the grace that continues to flow from it. Calvary was the Temple of the eternal sacrifice. When we take part in the Eucharist and receive the Lord's Body and Blood, we are in the heart of Jerusalem, embraced by its deepest spiritual significance.

Discipleship's learning curve can be sharp, and we may vacillate many times on the road. But there is never a good reason to give up. We, too, must continue on our way "today, tomorrow, and the following day." The Lord follows us when we walk away, listens to our protests and our fears, and feeds us with food that puts us right back where we need to be.

Celebrating Easter — set free by his love

At the beginning of Jesus' public ministry, John the Baptist pointed him out to two of his disciples. Jesus turned to them and asked, "What are you looking for?"

They said, "Where are you staying?" and Jesus replied, "Come, and you will see."

During Holy Week I find myself reflecting on one brief section in the Passion according to John which echoes that early encounter.

When Judas arrived at the garden with soldiers armed with lanterns and weapons, Jesus went out to greet them (see Jn 18:4-8).

"Whom are you looking for?" he asked. When they answered, "Jesus the Nazorean," he responded, "I AM." John the Evangelist is clear that Jesus did not say, "I am Jesus the Nazorean" — rather, he said, "I AM," God's own name which he revealed to Moses at the burning bush (see Ex 3:14).

Easter is the proper time to let Jesus look us straight in the eye and say, "What are you looking for? Whom are you looking for?"

Such questions strike at the heart, because they presuppose we are looking, that we are yearning, that we are reaching for something beyond ourselves. We are always doing just that, whether we realize it or not.

Who among us has not felt an interior longing, a longing we could not identify or understand, one that simply would not go away? Who among us could deny that at times we have just "gone looking" for nothing in particular, only to bump into the wrong things? Perhaps those wrong things frightened us — or worse, perhaps they did not. Who among us could deny that at times we have foolishly assumed that our yearning could be fulfilled by something that was not good for us?

Who of us has not gone looking for God, hoping that he was also looking for us?

Who of us has not gone looking for God, hoping that he was also looking for us?

"What are you looking for? Whom are you looking for?" Jesus asks. Whether or not we can put our finger on the answer, whether we have even figured out what we are looking for, Jesus' simple response to John's disciples is truly the answer for us all: "Come, and you will see."

Following after him will first awaken in us the deeper questions, the right questions. It will then uncover for us the wrong paths we have sometimes taken, to our embarrassment and shame. Most of all, following him will lead us to deeper faith. "Come, and you will see."

What did those who followed him — not those who were casual bystanders, but those who really followed him — end up seeing? They saw Jesus set people free.

They saw Jesus set sinners free from the wrong path, from guilt and shame. They saw him set the sick free from their illnesses and their banishment from normal life. They saw him set the angry free from their seething paralysis, the blind from their blindness, the hopeless from their despair, the prideful and self-possessed from their smugness. They saw regular folks — folks with no particular axe to grind, folks just trying to be good — discover the true path to happiness. They saw Jesus show another way, an alternative to the world's way of power and force, the way of love. They saw him set the dead free from death and bring them back to life.

But how did Jesus bring such freedom to those who went looking for him? The answer is in his passion and death. John the Evangelist tells us that in the garden when Jesus asked Judas and his companions again who they were looking for, they responded as they had before, "Jesus the Nazorean." But this time Jesus said something quite remarkable:

"I have told you that I AM. So if you are looking for me, let these men go."

"Let these men go." This brief phrase gives a hint of Jesus' atoning mission. It was as if he had said: "I will take their place. I will take upon myself their guilt, their sin, their sickness, their pride, their anger, their blindness, their exile, their hunger for power, their fear, their shame, their sentence of death . . . so that they may go free once and for all. Let them go. It is me you want."

Everything that Jesus took to the cross was sin or the outgrowth of sin, and it added up to death. Taking everything upon himself, Jesus carried it to Calvary, taking our place, the place of the guilty, so that we could go free. His heavenly Father raised him from the dead so that we would be free even of death.

Easter is the time of seeking and finding Jesus, of being set free by his love. It is a time to savor with both gratitude and trust the hand of eternal friendship God extends to us and to take our faith — our sight — seriously.

Come, and you will see.

Only Christ brings the peace that lasts

Ionce saw a TV commercial claiming that a certain mattress would provide "a lifetime of temporary relief." I laughed out loud. This mattress will ease your suffering for a lifetime, but only a few hours at a time. Forever temporarily — isn't that an oxymoron?

The commercial reflects a deep-seated cultural dynamic to which we can easily fall prey: the search for a quick fix to human suffering. In its extreme, this search leads to the misuse of alcohol, painkillers, sleeping pills, sex, money, gambling, and relationships, among other things.

The reckless search for relief in all the wrong places is a disaster in the making. Left unchecked, it spirals out of control, as one method of relief after another inevitably plays itself out, exposing its worthlessness. The search for temporary relief becomes an addiction, more powerful and more insidious than the original pain.

One of the tragedies of our cultural mindset is that many people settle for a lifetime of temporary relief. If they do not get lost in the reckless search, they may live in relative tranquility and never fall into serious sin; but they will never know what it means to be fully alive. Only God can bring the kind of healing, meaning, integration, and fulfillment for which we thirst. The Bible uses such words as "save," "redeem," "raise," "ransom," "rescue," and "free" to express what God has done for us. There is no mention of temporary relief, for that is far inferior to what God wants to give.

Suffering can be a source of strength, a vehicle of love, and an experience that helps us see how intimately Jesus has joined himself to us.

Modern medicine's capacity to cure many diseases and ease debilitating pain, both physical and emotional, is a true blessing. The fallacy inherent in the relentless search for temporary relief, however, is that any suffering is a hopelessly fruitless intrusion into otherwise carefree lives. In other words, once we get past all suffering, we can get back to living. Suffering is a mystery, to be sure, but it does not have to be fruitless. It can be a source of strength, a vehicle of love, and an experience that helps us see how intimately Jesus has joined himself to us.

In *Crossing the Threshold of Hope*, St. John Paul II wrote: "God is always on the side of the suffering. His omnipotence is manifested precisely in the fact that he freely accepted suffering. He could have chosen not to do so. He could have chosen to demonstrate his omnipotence even at the moment of the Crucifixion.... The fact that he stayed on the cross until the end, the fact that on the cross he could say, as do all who suffer: 'My God, my God, why have you forsaken me?' (Mk 15:34), has remained in human history the strongest argument. If the agony of the cross had not happened, the truth that God is love would have been unfounded."

Suffering and death entered the world as a result of sin, and only freedom from the power of evil can transform them. The Holy Father continued: "To save means to liberate from radical, ultimate evil.... Through the work of the redeemer death ceases to be an ultimate evil; it becomes subject to the power of life.... The world, which is capable of perfecting therapeutic techniques in various fields, does not have the power to liberate man from death.... Only God saves, and he saves the whole of humanity in Christ."

No Christian's life is without pain or suffering. But because of the Cross and Resurrection, suffering and death are no longer enslaved to the power of evil; they are freed by the power of life. Suffering can be a means of giving oneself to God, with Jesus, and it can bear fruit for others in him. Death is no longer an end but a means to ultimate union with God. Jesus shows us the way to the fruitfulness of suffering, to life in union with God: complete and childlike trust that God, who seems to have forsaken us, will give us the healing we seek . . . and more.

We must be on guard not to treat God as just another pain reliever, withdrawing to him only in times of trouble. God is not an analgesic or a Band-Aid. His grace does not kick in when the pain begins. He does not take up where our strength leaves off. He does not fill in the gaps we are unable to cover. God is life itself, and giving ourselves to him we find not temporary relief, but healing and peace, even in the midst of suffering.

Salvation is an event that has already taken place. The answer to the question, "Are you saved?" is an enthusiastic and unequivocal, "Yes!" Or as St. Paul writes in many places, because of baptism we are "in Christ Jesus." We are now subject to the power of life, not to the power of death. Everything — including our pain and suffering — is in Christ and will be used by him for good. "I have been crucified with Christ; yet I live, no longer I, but Christ lives in me" (Gal 2:19-20).

Those searching for a lifetime of temporary relief will not find it in God.

But those searching for God will find salvation, peace, and hope of the eternal brand, "In Christ Jesus," the kind nothing can shake or destroy.

"I have told you this so that you might have peace in me. In the world you will have trouble, but take courage, I have conquered the world" (Jn 16:33).

Through the Cross
all is made new

Several years ago I had the privilege of standing in a pulpit sculpted from stone in the early sixteenth century. A Spanish inscription, dated 1520, reads, "Here the holy Gospel had its beginning in this new world." It was a rare opportunity to reflect on the hundreds of thousands of people who have heard the Gospel preached from that pulpit in the past five hundred years.

A few yards away stands a massive baptismal font, which according to tradition was carved from a stone that had once been used for human sacrifice. It was there, five hundred years ago, that four native chieftains were baptized into the new religion, Christianity.

The pulpit and font are found in the Cathedral of Tlaxcala, a small town about seventy miles east of Mexico City. Tlaxcala was part of the very first diocese established in Mexico, and its cathedral, with a beautiful cedar ceiling carved in the Moorish style, holds special prominence in Church history. It is fascinating to realize that the Gospel preached five hundred years ago from the pulpit in that cathedral is still being handed on, generation after generation.

Back in 1520, Europeans considered uncharted territory across the Atlantic the "New World," and Mexico was "New Spain." Missionaries accompanied the early explorers bearing the word of God and the sacraments of the Church, because they knew it was Christ who would truly make all things and all people "new." The pulpit in Tlaxcala is important because it represents their pioneering missionary spirit, but even more because it represents the power of the word of God.

On the cross, Jesus spoke only a few words, but the message he proclaimed there brought fulfillment and clarity to everything he had said and done to that point.

During Holy Week, we Catholics remember the cross of Jesus — his suffering, his courage, his sacrifice, his generosity, his compassion, his mercy, his innocence, his death, his "new commandment" — his love. It is not that he was merely a good man, or even an extraordinarily great man worthy of imitation. He was and is the Son of God, sent by the Father for our salvation. He is the Word of God, spoken with the breath of the Holy Spirit. He is the innocent one, who took on the sins of the guilty because it was not within our power to forgive or save ourselves. He is the beginning of the new creation, the One in whom everything and everyone begins again, afresh, anew.

St. Augustine once said, "The cross was not only the instrument of Christ's suffering but also the pulpit of his teachings." On the cross, Jesus spoke only a few words, but the message he proclaimed there brought fulfillment and clarity to everything he had said and done to that point. Stripped of everything and painfully paralyzed by the nails of his cross, he could not preach and minister as had been his custom. But what he proclaimed from the cross was good news for our salvation: "Trust my Father. Give everything to him. He will destroy the power of death in you."

Cardinal Miloslav Vlk of Prague, Czech Republic, once spoke about the years during which he was stripped of his priestly ministry by the Communist regime, forced to take a job as a laborer, and not allowed to associate publicly with other priests.

He was confused, broken, lonely, and full of doubt. Gathering in secret with a group of brother priests each week, he began to realize that what had seemed such a desperate hardship actually gave him profound insight into the priesthood.

He wrote: "It was an immense joy to discover that Jesus arrived at the climax of his priesthood when, nailed to the cross, he could not walk, perform miracles, nor preach, but — abandoned — suffered in silence. Nevertheless it is in this way that he has saved us. I understood and found in him my deepest identity, which filled me with joy and peace."

As the early Christians reflected on the Cross, they realized that the promises of the ages came to fulfillment in Jesus Christ: hope for the poor, healing for the sick, forgiveness for the sinner, release from confinement, peace among people, reconciliation with God.

His message spoke eloquently, because it was the message of humble abandonment, of giving of self, to the Father. In Jesus, we see the saving power of his heavenly Father clearly, without the slightest blur or blemish, because he trusted in his Father utterly and completely, without reserve. God raised him on high, and with him all of us.

Creation is new in Jesus Christ, the new Adam through whom the Father has started afresh, re-creating the world and us just as we were meant to be from the beginning.

A new world, a new creation, a new heaven, a new earth, a new humanity, a new heart, a new spirit, a new commandment, a new woman, a new man — all because of Jesus. This Easter, at our pulpits and baptismal fonts we proclaim to future generations: "Here the holy Gospel made new, God's sons and daughters, through the saving Word, the cleansing water, the consecrating chrism, and the body and blood of the Lord. Here we, too, are born again."